100 EASY RECIPES

IN JARS

BONNIE SCOTT

CONTENTS

BONNIE SCOTT

100 Easy Recipes In Jars

A handcrafted gift, created especially for the recipient, is truly a gift that shows how much you care. If your gift is brimming with yummy goodness, that makes it ever so much better! Create tasty and appetizing mixes for family and friends that can be used throughout the year. It's like giving love in a jar.

With recipes for everything from cookies, breads and soups to snacks and drinks, there will be a fun and festive package for everyone on your gift list this Christmas and all year long.

These recipes combine the ease of a mix with the wholesome goodness of cooking from scratch. Use the freshest and finest ingredients to make a gift that will be appreciated long after the presents are opened and the bustle of the holidays is over.

The helpful hints for assembling your creations make this project a breeze, and the colorful label and recipe templates will make your gift a colorful and memorable one.

Filling Your Jar

Since you are using clear jars, layer the ingredients attractively. Plan the order of filling the container to make attractive contrasts of colors and textures. If your ingredients don't quite fill the jar, add extra nuts, chocolate chips or other candies that are part of the recipe for a full to the top look.

Remember that finely ground items like sugar and flour will filter down through larger items like nuts and chocolate chips, so plan the most finely ground items for the bottom layers of your sand art.

Double check the size of jar you will require to hold all the ingredients. Wide mouth jars are far easier to fill than the narrow mouth variety. One quart or one liter jars fit most recipes, but you may have to pack them tightly.

If you are adding dusty or crumbly products like cocoa, ground nuts or confectioners' sugar, wipe the inside of the jar before adding other ingredients to keep it looking clean and fresh.

Pack each layer tightly to conserve space. Use a flat-bottomed utensil or a juice glass that fits through the mouth of the jar to compress a layer before adding the next ingredient.

Ingredients

Make sure you use the freshest ingredients, and don't scrimp by using inferior quality products. These gift jars are meant to have a fairly long shelf life, so it's important to use fresh ingredients that will last.

Tiny plastic zippered bags are inexpensive and available at the candy or jewelry center of a craft shop. If you know your jar will be sitting in storage for a while, use these to package baking soda or baking powder, as they lose their potency quickly. Tuck them in the center of the jar so they are hidden and don't ruin your sand art design.

Brown sugar hardens quickly. Package it in a plastic zipper bag or small plastic container, or make sure the recipient knows to use the mix within a few weeks, as it can become rock hard. The brown sugar can be chiseled out, but that is probably not what you want your recipient to have to do. Nuts do not have a long shelf life so be sure to purchase fresh nuts.

 If you are making up your jars ahead of time, just store them in a dry, cool, dark area and they should stay fresh. If you use fresh ingredients, the jars should be usable for up to six months.

Decorating Your Jars

After you've packed the jars, it's time for decorating fun. Choose colors that will coordinate with the recipient's kitchen décor, or select colors to celebrate the season.

Scraps of patterned fabrics are inexpensive and you only need a small square or two to cover your jar lid. Use pinking shears to make a zigzag border for a country look. If you use a loosely woven fabric, unravel the edges to create fringe for a shabby chic look. Two squares of fabric, turned 90 degrees from each other, gives a double punch of color.

Use a thin rubber band to secure the fabric in place on the lid. You can now fuss with your fabric to get the positioning just right before adding the ribbon, which will cover the rubber band.

Use ribbon, twine or a leather cord to tie around your jar lid. Natural or paper raffia is also available at local craft shops and available in many colors. Use your pinking shears to cut narrow strips of fabric to use as your ribbon, or use rickrack or lace to tie up your gift.

You can also use bits of lace, rick rack or other festive trims and buttons to add texture and color. Your glue stick is your friend and it's easy to add fun embellishments to give your gift a designer look. Double sided tape can also easily adhere your trim to the container.

Add custom labels, hang tags and recipe cards to your gifts. You can customize them with personal messages, or create generic tags that can be used for any occasion. Use a hole punch to make a hole to hang your tag with string or ribbon.

Other Fun Filled Containers

There are lots of other options for decorative gift containers. Use a heavy duty plastic freezer bag to hold all the ingredients, and pop them in a decorative tin container or cookie jar. Bundle the bag up in colorful cellophane and tie with a bow. Add it to a basket lined with a kitchen towel. You can also sew a cloth drawstring bag in holiday fabric to hold your gift, and tie it up with a bit of holly and your hanging gift tag. Jars are heavy for mailing, so the plastic freezer bag is a great alternative for sending cookie mix to relatives.

Get the kids involved. Buy inexpensive cardboard gift containers at a local craft shop, or save lidded oatmeal containers. Let the children paint and decoupage the outside of the gift boxes, then fill with a bagged mix. You can add your own label and recipe card to their masterpiece.

For a new bride or a young person setting up their first kitchen, place your cellophane, ribbon decorated gift in a great mixing bowl. Add a wooden spoon with a bow to complete the gift. To make a complete baking set, include a cookie sheet, timer, measuring cup and spoons.

Tie a set of cookie cutters with a ribbon, and attach it to a sugar cookie mix jar. For a family gift, wrap your cookie mix jar in a kitchen towel to protect the glass. Place it in a festive new cookie jar. Mom will appreciate the new canister and towel, while the kids enjoy the fresh baked cookies.

Other ideas for cookie gift jars might include pairing cookie mix and cocoa mix jars in a basket with a small bag of mini-marshmallows. Add a family favorite DVD movie for a perfect evening at home gift.

Dip the bowl ends of plastic spoons in melted chocolate. Scatter with colored sugar or candy sprinkles, and tie up one or two in a piece of cellophane. Attach to a gift jar of cocoa or flavored coffee mix with a decorative ribbon.

Another taste treat to add to a beverage mix is homemade biscotti. Dip one end in melted chocolate chips or chocolate bark. Tie up a nice selection with cellophane and attach to your gift jar.

Add a jar of cocoa or coffee mix, a pair of cute ceramic mugs and a holiday CD to a gift basket. You could purchase a small serving tray, tie the entire set in cellophane and add a big bow to the top.

Other Recipe In A Jar Uses

Recipes in a jar are great items for fund raising. Use them for silent auctions, raffles, church bazaars and craft shows.

If your child's school has a Santa's Store for students to buy gifts for their parents and relatives, recipes in a jar are great ideas for kids to purchase as Christmas gifts.

Jars that are being sold should have generic gift tags and labels so the giver can personalize them.

These ready-to-use jars also make great emergency gifts for unexpected guests and last-minute additions to your gift-giving list.

A mix in a jar is also a thoughtful 'welcome to the neighborhood' present for a new neighbor.

Jars are also popular as wedding favors or wedding table decorations. Personalize the jars with the names of your guests and show off your creative side at the same time. Wedding favor jars are popular and help hold down the cost of a wedding. Have a cute personalized label professionally printed with the names and wedding date.

Hints And Tips

Fill jars to the top to eliminate as much air as possible and to avoid the possibility of disturbing the layers when the jar is moved.

If the ingredients are packaged in a plastic bag, squeeze out as much air as possible before sealing it. This will help to keep the contents fresh.

Place the finest ground ingredients at the bottom of the jar. This includes items like sugar, flour and powdered sugar. If placed above coarse items like nuts or chocolate chips they will seep down through the layers, and your gift will not retain its sand art look.

Store gift jars in a cool, dark and dry area. The ingredients will remain usable up to six months, provided the ingredients are fresh. Placing the jar for display on a sunny windowsill or counter will significantly reduce the shelf life of your mix.

You should package baking powder and baking soda separately in sealed bags to ensure freshness, if the jar will not be used right away.

Mark your gift with the giving date. The recipient won't have to worry about the ingredients becoming stale if they know the date the jar originated.

Putting the Jars Together

STEP BY STEP

Fabric Top

I like using 2 pieces of fabric on the top of quart jars, but just one piece also works nicely. I use from a 6" square to a 9" square. Use a 6 or 6 1/2" square or even smaller if you want the top layer in your jar to be viewable. I even use a 6" square for the smaller half-pint jars. In the cover photo, the red and green dotted fabrics are 6" squares. One square in the red dotted fabric, one in the green dotted fabric, placed at angles to each other. The M&M's® layer shows up nicely with the shorter fabric.

The red dot fabric on the cover is a 6 1/2" square. The red dot fabric combined with the white fabric hang nice but farther from the top of the jar by being just 1/2" longer.

The brown and teal fabrics on the cover are 9" squares. They create a more dramatic cover on the top of the jar. This longer top dresses up the jar when you don't have anything especially colorful to show off in the jar (like M&M's®) or when the whole jar is mixed up anyway, as with some of the snacks.

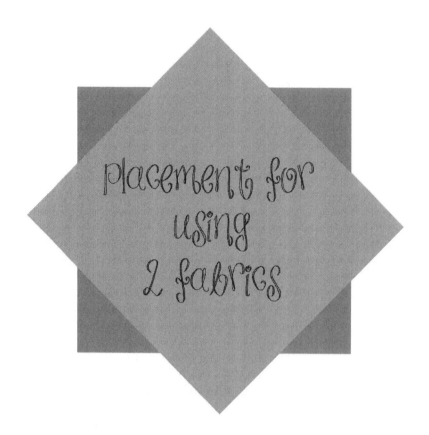

Ribbon and Decorative Trim

I use a thin rubber band about 3" long around the top of the jar over the fabric before adding the ribbon or trim. The thin, loose rubber band will allow the fabric to be manipulated and straightened before applying the trim, yet hold the fabric in place.

Thin ribbons work best, but if they are too thin, the rubber band may show through. 3/8" ribbon is what I use on most of the jars. 1/8" decorative trim does look pretty but may show some of the rubber band. Use approximately 30 inches of ribbon for each top.

Thin lengths of jute also look cute, especially on homespun fabrics. Raffia is another medium that can be used for the bow.

Some jars in this book do not actually have fabric adorning the top, but just have decorative trim wound around the lid. Double sided tape works great for holding the trim in place if just a few pieces of tape are placed on the jar lid rim before winding the trim around.

All the ribbons, trim and fabrics used in this book are available at either Hobby Lobby stores or Joann fabric stores.

Labels, Hang Tags, Recipe Cards

Each recipe in this book has 3 pages of labels, tags and recipe cards available to print out. Since there are 100 recipes, there are 300 pages of labels, way too many to include in this book. So the labels are available on the internet and can be accessed with your computer and printed.

There is a large variety of holiday labels, everyday labels and recipe cards. Also the jars are available for viewing on the web page in color.

Ideas for attaching the recipe cards to the jars:

- Attach to the jar fabric or ribbon with a safety pin
- Punch a hole in the recipe card and tie it to the ribbon with jute or ribbon
- Roll the recipe card up like a scroll and tie it with jute or ribbon
- If the recipe is short and sweet, just print out the small recipe card and stick it to the back of the jar. I have made labels just for that purpose when the recipe is brief.

The internet address to access all the recipes' labels, tags and recipe cards is:

www.NorthPoleChristmas.com/jars.html

Visual Jar Filling

Putting the ingredients in a jar:

Supplies that are not necessary but make jarring a whole lot easier if you are making more than one or two jars are:

- canning funnel

- bean masher or other utensil that is flat on the bottom with a handle

The canning jars are available at Walmart and canning funnels are stocked by the jars.

Approximately 4 3/4 cups will fit in a quart jar if it is packed tightly and 4 cups if it cannot be packed as with nuts. 2 cups of snacks (unpacked) will fit in a pint jar.

The following pages are the basic steps you will go through in filling a jar. The jar I am filling in the examples is for the Holiday Cranberry Cookies.

Start by placing the funnel over the jar.

Next the flour mixture is usually added. It is the messiest layer and the flour will seep through any other layer (like raisins) that you cannot pack tightly, so I normally place it first in the jar.

Pack the flour mixture with the bean masher. The flour may make a mess on the inside of the jar and if it does, after packing the flour, just use a paper towel and clean the inside of the jar.

Next a packable layer like the brown sugar is nice to add. It keeps the flour where it is supposed to be in the jar.

Now pack the brown sugar firmly.

My bean masher actually has a scalloped pattern on the edge and sometimes I get that cute pattern on the brown sugar edge.

Next I added the white sugar.

Pack the sugar layer firmly. Just pack each layer as you go unless the layer is an ingredient like chocolate chips. Even the chip layer can be pushed down lightly.

Dried cranberries are added next. They can be packed a little, but don't pack too hard. You don't want cranberry juice in the jar.

Last in this recipe to add are vanilla chips. They will sit loosely on top of everything else in the jar. It is smart to put nuts, chips or fruit as the final layer, in case your packing was not as firm as you thought and you run out of room. You can always put just a little less of those ingredients in the jar or add more if you have the room.

And voilà, the final jar is ready for sealing and decorating. For sealing, just be sure the metal lid is clean, especially the rubber coating along the edge. Clean the top rim of the jar before placing the lid on, then add the ring and tighten. This is not actually a sealing process as in canning but will keep your ingredients fresh for quite a while.

The final finished project – Holiday Cranberry Cookies

Cookies

Most of the cookie recipes yield about 24 cookies, give or take a few depending on the ingredients in the jar and the size of the cookie.

Kris Kringle Granola Cookies

1 1/4 cups flour
3/4 teaspoon salt
3/4 teaspoon baking soda
1/2 cup sugar
1/2 cup packed brown sugar
1 1/4 cups granola
1/2 cup chocolate chips
1/2 cup M & M's
1/4 cup walnuts
Jar – Wide mouth quart glass canning jar

Combine the flour, salt and baking soda. Layer in jar in this order: flour mixture, granola, brown sugar, sugar, M&M's®, chocolate chips and finally, walnuts. Pack each layer well and it will all fit. Seal jar.

Attach the following recipe to the jar:

Kris Kringle Granola Cookies

2/3 cup margarine, softened
3/4 teaspoon vanilla
1 egg

Preheat oven to 350 degrees F. Combine the margarine, vanilla and egg in a bowl. Add the cookie mix from the jar to the bowl and stir until well blended. Line a cookie sheet with parchment paper or use ungreased cookie sheet. Drop dough by rounded spoonfuls and bake for 10 to 12 minutes. Makes 2 dozen cookies.

Chocolate Dreams Cookie Mix

1 package brownie mix (19.8 ounces)
1/4 cup flour
2 cups peanut butter chips
Jar – Wide mouth quart glass canning jar

In the jar, layer the brownie mix, flour and peanut butter chips, packing each layer. Seal the jar.

Attach the following recipe to the jar:

Chocolate Dreams Cookies

2 eggs
3 tablespoons water
1/4 cup vegetable oil

Preheat oven to 350 degrees F. In a medium bowl, combine the eggs, water and vegetable oil. Add the jar of cookie mix and stir until blended. Lightly grease a cookie sheet. Drop dough by the spoonful on the cookie sheet and bake for 8 to 9 minutes. Makes 2 dozen.

Santa's M&M Cookie Mix

2 cups flour
1 teaspoon baking soda
1 teaspoon baking powder
1 teaspoon salt
1 cup brown sugar (not packed)
1/2 cup white sugar
1 1/4 cups M&M's® candies
Jar – Wide mouth quart glass canning jar

Mix the flour with the baking soda, baking powder and salt. Layer the ingredients in the jar in this order: flour mixture, brown sugar, sugar, M&M's®. Pack each layer firmly in jar so all the ingredients will fit. Be sure to put the M&M's® on top so they can be separated for the recipe below.

 Attach the following recipe to the jar:

Santa's M&M Cookies

1 cup margarine, softened
2 eggs
2 teaspoons vanilla

Preheat oven to 350 degrees F. Mix the vanilla, margarine and eggs in a large bowl. Set aside half of the M&M's® in the cookie mix jar. Pour the rest of the jar mixture into a large bowl and stir until mixed. Add the margarine mixture to cookie mix and stir until completely blended. (Be sure the margarine is cooled before adding to mix or the colored outside of the M&M's® will melt off.)

Lightly grease a cookie sheet. Drop dough by the spoonfuls on the cookie sheet and push a few M&M's® on top of each cookie. Bake for 9 to 10 minutes until cookies are just golden brown on the edges. Makes 3 dozen cookies.

Cinnamon Oatmeal Cookie Mix

3/4 cup flour
1/4 teaspoon baking soda
1 1/4 teaspoons cinnamon
1/2 teaspoon salt
2/3 cup packed brown sugar
1/4 cup white sugar
1 3/4 cups quick cooking oats
1/2 cup chopped walnuts
Jar – Wide mouth quart glass canning jar

Mix together the flour, baking soda, salt and cinnamon. In the jar, place the flour mixture and pack, then add the rest of the ingredients on top.

Attach the following recipe to the jar:

Cinnamon Oatmeal Cookies

1/2 cup butter, softened
1 egg
1 1/4 teaspoon vanilla extract

Preheat oven to 325 degrees F. In a large bowl, mix together the butter, egg and vanilla. Pour the mixture from the jar into the bowl and mix well. Drop dough by the spoonfuls on ungreased cookie sheet. Bake for 12 minutes.

Dark Chocolate Chunk Cookie Mix

These are absolutely the best cookies for any dark chocolate lover. The recipe below will fill a quart jar to the brim, so be sure to pack each layer well, even the chocolate.

1 3/4 cups flour
1/4 teaspoon salt
1 teaspoon baking powder
1 teaspoon baking soda
1/2 cup cocoa powder
7 ounces dark chocolate (1 giant candy bar or 2 regular candy bars)
3/4 cup brown sugar
1/2 cup sugar
Jar – Wide mouth quart glass canning jar

Break chocolate bars into chunks. Mix together the flour, salt, baking powder and baking soda. Layer the ingredients in the jar in this order: flour mixture, dark chocolate chunks, brown sugar, cocoa powder, white sugar. Pack each layer firmly in jar.

 Attach the following recipe to the jar:

Dark Chocolate Chunk Cookies

3/4 cup soft margarine
1 egg, slightly beaten
2 teaspoons vanilla

Preheat oven to 350 degrees F. Mix the egg, margarine and vanilla in a large bowl. Empty the jar of cookie mix in the bowl. Stir until well blended. Line a baking sheet with parchment paper or lightly grease. Drop the dough by the spoonful on the baking sheet and bake for 9 to 11 minutes until just golden brown on the edges. Makes 4 dozen cookies.

Dark Chocolate Chunk Cookies

Chewy Raisin Cookie Mix

1 cup flour
1/2 teaspoon ground nutmeg
3/4 teaspoon ground cinnamon
1/2 teaspoon salt
3/4 teaspoon baking soda
1 cup packed brown sugar
1/2 cup raisins
2 1/4 cups rolled oats
Jar – Wide mouth quart glass canning jar

Add the salt, cinnamon, nutmeg and baking soda to the flour and mix. In the jar, layer the flour mixture, sugar, oats and finally, the raisins on top, being sure to pack each layer except the raisins.

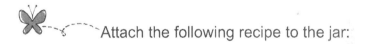Attach the following recipe to the jar:

Chewy Raisin Cookies

3/4 cup margarine, softened
1 egg, slightly beaten
1 teaspoon of vanilla
2 teaspoons of honey

Preheat oven to 350 degrees F. Mix the butter, egg, honey and vanilla in a large bowl. Add the contents of the jar into the bowl. Stir until well blended. Drop by spoonfuls on a lightly greased cookie sheet. Bake 10 to 14 minutes or until cookies begin to brown.

Chocolate Cherry Cookie Mix

1 1/2 cups flour
1/8 teaspoon salt
1/2 cup brown sugar
1 1/2 cup chocolate chips
Small jar of maraschino cherries (about 24)
Jar - 1 wide mouth quart canning jar

Mix the flour and salt together. Layer the flour mixture, the brown sugar, then chocolate chips in the jar. Be sure to put the chocolate chips on top so they can be used separately in the recipe below. Give the jar of cherries along with the quart canning jar.

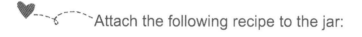Attach the following recipe to the jar:

Chocolate Cherry Cookies

1/2 cup margarine
1 teaspoon vanilla

Preheat oven to 350 degrees F. Remove the chocolate chips from the jar and set aside. Mix the vanilla and margarine together. Add the rest of the dry ingredients from the jar (all except the chocolate chips) and mix well.

Drain the jar of maraschino cherries. Put a chocolate chip

inside each cherry, then wrap about a teaspoon of dough around the cherry. Bake on an ungreased cookie sheet for 12 to 15 minutes. Melt the remainder of the chocolate chips in the microwave and dip the top of cookies in the melted chocolate.

Gingerbread Cookie Mix

Tie one or more cookie cutters to the jar for this recipe.

3 1/2 cups flour
1/2 teaspoon salt
1 teaspoon baking soda
1 teaspoon ground ginger
1/2 teaspoon ground allspice
1/2 teaspoon ground cinnamon
1/2 teaspoon ground cloves
1/2 cup packed brown sugar
Gingerbread boy cookie cutter
Jar – Wide mouth quart glass canning jar

Mix all the spices, baking soda and the flour. Layer the flour mixture in the jar, then the brown sugar, packing each layer.

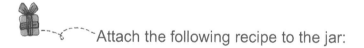Attach the following recipe to the jar:

Gingerbread Cookies

3/4 cup dark molasses
3 tablespoons shortening
1/3 cup cold water
Can of chocolate or vanilla frosting

Mix together the molasses, water and shortening in a large bowl. Empty the jar of cookie mix into the bowl and stir until well blended. Cover and refrigerate for 1 hour or longer.

Preheat oven to 350 degrees F. Roll dough to 1/4" thick on a lightly floured surface. Cut into shapes with cookie cutter. Lightly grease a baking sheet and bake 10 to 15 minutes. Decorate with icing.

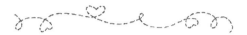

Gingerbread Cookies

Santa's Sugar Cookie Mix

This is another jar that would be cute with cookie cutters added to your ribbon or bow.

3 cups flour
1 teaspoon baking powder
1/2 teaspoon salt
1 1/2 cup granulated sugar
Jar - 1 wide mouth quart canning jar

Mix the flour, baking powder and salt together. Layer the flour mixture, then the sugar in the jar. Be sure to add the sugar as the last layer so it can be separated for the recipe below.

Attach the following recipe to the jar:

Santa's Sugar Cookies

1 cup margarine, softened
3 eggs
2 teaspoons vanilla extract

Preheat oven to 375 degrees F. Pour the top sugar layer from the jar into a large bowl. Add the margarine and cream until smooth. Add vanilla and eggs and stir well. Stir in the rest of the mixture from the jar. Refrigerate dough for one hour or overnight. Roll the cold dough thinly on parchment paper or a floured surface. Cut with cookie cutters and bake on ungreased cookie sheet for 6 to 8 minutes or until lightly golden in color.

Tip: Roll the dough out on parchment paper, then use cookie cutters to cut the shapes. Just remove the excess dough from around the cutouts. Then the parchment paper is ready to slide onto a cookie sheet to bake.

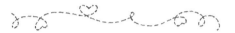

Santa's Sugar Cookies

Chocolate Chip Cookie Mix

1 teaspoon salt
1 teaspoon baking soda
2 cups all-purpose flour
3/4 cup brown sugar, packed
3/4 cup granulated sugar
1 1/4 cups semi-sweet chocolate chips
Jar – Wide mouth quart glass canning jar

Mix the flour, salt and baking soda together, then layer the flour mixture, sugars and the chocolate chips on top, being sure to pack each layer firmly so it will all fit.

 Attach the following recipe to the jar:

Chocolate Chip Cookies

1 cup butter, softened
2 eggs
1 teaspoon vanilla
Optional – 1 cup chopped nuts

Preheat oven to 375 degrees F. Cream butter, eggs and vanilla in a large bowl. Empty the jar of cookie mix into the bowl. Stir until well blended. Lightly grease a baking sheet. Bake 8 to 10 minutes or until light brown.

Oatmeal Chocolate Chip Cookie Mix

1 cup flour
1/4 teaspoon salt
1/2 teaspoon baking soda
1/2 teaspoon cinnamon
1/2 cup packed brown sugar
1/4 cup white sugar
1 1/4 cups rolled oats
1 cup semi-sweet chocolate chips
2/3 cup chopped walnuts

Jar – Wide mouth quart glass canning jar

Mix the flour, salt, cinnamon and baking soda together. Layer in the jar - flour mixture, sugars, oats and the chocolate chips and walnuts on top.

Attach the following recipe to the jar:

Oatmeal Chocolate Chip Cookies

1 egg
1/2 cup butter, softened
1 teaspoon vanilla extract

Preheat oven to 350 degrees F. Cream butter, egg and vanilla in a large bowl. Empty the jar of cookie mix into the bowl. Stir until well blended. Drop by spoonfuls on an ungreased cookie sheet. Bake 9 to 10 minutes or until light brown.

Peanut Butter Chunk Cookie Mix

1 3/4 cups flour
1 teaspoon baking soda
1/2 teaspoon salt
1/2 cup white sugar
1/2 cup packed brown sugar
8 Reese's peanut butter cups cut into 1/2" pieces
Jar – Wide mouth quart glass canning jar

Mix together the flour, salt and baking soda. Layer the ingredients in the jar - flour mixture, brown sugar, white sugar, peanut butter cup pieces.

 Attach the following recipe to the jar:

Peanut Butter Chunk Cookies

1 egg, slightly beaten
1 teaspoon vanilla
1/2 cup margarine, softened
1/2 cup peanut butter

Preheat oven to 375 degrees F. Remove peanut butter cups from the jar. Empty the rest of the cookie mix into a large mixing bowl and stir until well blended. Add the margarine, egg, peanut butter and vanilla to the mix and stir well. Add the peanut butter cups.

Shape into 1" balls or use a small cookie scoop. Bake for 8

to 10 minutes until cookies are just golden brown on the edges. Makes 2 1/2 dozen cookies.

Holiday Cranberry Cookie Mix

1 3/4 cups flour
1/2 teaspoon baking soda
1/2 cup brown sugar, packed
1/2 cup granulated sugar
1 cup dried cranberries
3/4 cup white chocolate baking chips
Jar – Wide mouth quart glass canning jar

Mix the flour and baking soda together. Layer in the jar - flour mixture, brown sugar, sugar, cranberries and white chips. Pack each layer well. Seal jar.

Attach the following recipe to the jar:

Holiday Cranberry Cookies

1 egg
1 teaspoon vanilla
1/2 cup margarine, softened

Preheat oven to 375 degrees F. Mix together the egg, vanilla and margarine in a large bowl. Add the contents of the jar and mix well. Lightly grease a cookie sheet. Drop by heaping spoonfuls on cookie sheet. Bake for 8 to 10 minutes.

Chocolate Covered Banana Cookie Mix

2 cups flour
1/4 teaspoon baking soda
1/2 teaspoon salt
1 teaspoon baking powder
1/2 cup brown sugar, packed
1/4 cup white sugar
2 cups semi-sweet chocolate chips
Jar – Wide mouth quart glass canning jar

Mix together the flour, baking soda, salt and baking powder. In the jar, layer the flour mixture, brown sugar, white sugar, then the chocolate chips, packing each layer. Seal the jar.

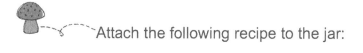Attach the following recipe to the jar:

Chocolate Covered Banana Cookies

1/2 cup butter, softened
2 eggs
1 teaspoon vanilla extract
1 cup ripe bananas, mashed

Preheat oven to 400 degrees F. Mix the butter, eggs and vanilla. Add the mashed bananas. Next add the contents of the jar and stir until well mixed. Drop by spoonfuls on greased cookie sheets. Bake for 12 to 15 minutes.

Vanilla Chip Cookie Mix

1 cup flour
1/4 teaspoon salt
1/2 teaspoon baking soda
1/2 cup sugar
1/4 cup brown sugar, packed
1 cup white chocolate chips
1/2 cup flaked coconut
1 cup Macadamia nuts, chopped
Jar - 1 wide mouth quart canning jar

Mix the flour, baking soda and salt together. Layer the flour mixture, brown sugar, white sugar, coconut, nuts and white chocolate chips in the jar. Seal jar.

Attach the following recipe to the jar:

Vanilla Chip Cookies

1/2 cup margarine, softened
1 teaspoon vanilla
1 egg

Preheat oven to 375 degrees F. Mix together the margarine, vanilla and egg. Add the contents of the jar and stir well. Drop by spoonfuls onto ungreased cookie sheets. Bake for 12 minutes or until golden.

Krispies Cookie Mix

1 3/4 cups flour
1/2 teaspoon salt
1/2 teaspoon cream of tartar
1/2 teaspoon baking soda
1/2 cup granulated sugar
1/2 cup brown sugar
1/2 cup Rice Krispies
1/2 cup oatmeal
1/2 cup coconut
1/4 cup chopped walnuts
Jar – Wide mouth quart glass canning jar

Mix the flour, salt, cream of tartar and baking soda together in a bowl. Place the flour mixture in a jar, then the brown sugar and white sugar and add the rest of the ingredients in any order. Seal jar.

Attach the following recipe to the jar:

Krispies Cookies

1 cup margarine
1 cup corn oil or vegetable oil
2 eggs
1 teaspoon vanilla

Preheat oven to 350 degrees F. Mix together the eggs,

margarine, oil and vanilla. Add the ingredients from the jar and mix well. Drop by tablespoonful's on ungreased cookie sheet. Bake for 12 minutes - don't brown.

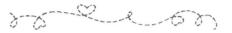

Snickerdoodles Cookie Mix

2 3/4 cups flour
1/4 teaspoon salt
1 teaspoon baking soda
2 teaspoons cream of tartar
1 1/2 cups white sugar
Jar – Wide mouth quart glass canning jar

Combine the flour, salt, cream of tartar and baking soda. Pack the flour mixture in the jar and add the sugar on top. Seal jar.

Attach the following recipe to the jar:

Snickerdoodle Cookies

1 cup margarine or butter
2 eggs
2 tablespoons white sugar
2 teaspoons cinnamon

Preheat oven to 400 degrees F. In a large bowl, mix together the butter and eggs. Add the contents of the jar to the bowl and mix well. In a separate bowl, mix together the white sugar and cinnamon. Shape the dough into 1 1/2" balls and then roll the balls in the cinnamon sugar. Bake for 8 to 10 minutes, until lightly brown.

Snickerdoodle Cookies

Chocolate Coconut Cookie Mix

3/4 cup flour
1/4 teaspoon salt
1/2 teaspoon baking soda
1/2 cup packed brown sugar
1/4 cup white sugar
1 1/2 cups rolled oats
1 cup semi-sweet chocolate chips
1/2 cup shredded coconut
Jar – Wide mouth quart glass canning jar

Mix the flour, salt and baking soda together. In a jar, layer the flour mixture, brown sugar, white sugar, oats, chocolate chips and coconut, packing each layer. Seal the jar.

 Attach the following recipe to the jar:

Chocolate Coconut Cookies

1/2 cup butter, softened
1 egg
1 tablespoon milk
1 teaspoon vanilla extract

Preheat oven to 350 degrees. Mix together the butter, egg, milk and vanilla. Add the cookie mix from the jar and stir until well blended. Drop by spoonfuls on greased cookie sheets. Bake for 7 to 10 minutes.

Noel Toffee Cookie Mix

1 1/2 cups flour
1/2 teaspoon baking soda
1/2 teaspoon salt
3/4 cup brown sugar, packed
1 1/2 cup toffee baking bits (or Heath toffee bits)
1/2 cup semi-sweet chocolate chips
1/2 cup chopped walnuts or pecans
Jar – Wide mouth quart glass canning jar

Combine the flour, salt and baking soda. Layer in jar - flour mixture, brown sugar, toffee baking bits, chocolate chips and nuts. Pack each layer well and seal jar.

Attach the following recipe to the jar:

Noel Toffee Cookies

1/2 cup margarine
1 egg
1 teaspoon vanilla extract

Preheat oven to 350 degrees F. In a large bowl, mix margarine, egg, and vanilla. Add the contents of the jar and mix well. Drop by spoonfuls on a lightly greased cookie sheet. Press down on each cookie a bit. Bake about 12 to 15 minutes. Makes 18 cookies.

Oatmeal M&M Cookie Mix

2 1/3 cups rolled oats
1 teaspoon baking soda
1/4 cup M&M's®
1/3 cup semi-sweet chocolate chips
1/2 cup white sugar
2/3 cup packed brown sugar
Jar – Wide mouth quart glass canning jar

Mix the oats and baking soda together and put in jar. Pack down firmly. Add the rest of the ingredients in this order - M&M's®, chocolate chips, brown sugar and white sugar. Seal jar.

Attach the following recipe to the jar:

Oatmeal M&M Cookies

1/4 cup butter or margarine
1/4 teaspoon vanilla
2 eggs
2/3 cup peanut butter

Preheat oven to 350 degrees F. In a large bowl, mix together butter, vanilla, eggs and peanut butter. Add all the ingredients from the jar. Shape dough into 1" balls. Bake on a lightly greased cookie sheet for 10 to 12 minutes.

Crunchy Cookie Mix

1 1/4 cup flour
1/2 teaspoon baking soda
1/2 teaspoon baking powder
1 cup oatmeal
1/2 cup white sugar
1/2 cup brown sugar, packed
3/4 cup corn flakes
1/4 cup coconut
1/2 cup salted peanuts
Jar – Wide mouth quart glass canning jar

Mix the flour, baking powder and baking soda together. In the jar, layer the flour mixture, then all the rest of the ingredients. Seal the jar.

 Attach the following recipe to the jar:

Crunchy Cookies

1 egg
1/2 teaspoon vanilla
3/4 cup margarine, melted

Preheat oven to 350 degrees F. Mix together the egg, vanilla and margarine in a large bowl. Add the contents of the jar and mix well. Drop by spoonfuls on an ungreased cookie sheet. Bake for 8 to 10 minutes.

Cappuccino Noel Balls Mix

1 3/4 cups all-purpose flour
1/2 teaspoon salt
1/4 cup unsweetened cocoa powder
1 tablespoon instant coffee granules
1/2 cup white sugar
2 cups finely chopped pecans
Jar - wide mouth quart canning jar

Stir together the flour, salt, cocoa powder and instant coffee.
Layer in jar: flour mixture, sugar and pecans.

Attach the following recipe to the jar:

Cappuccino Noel Balls

1 cup butter softened
2 teaspoons vanilla extract
1 cup confectioners' sugar for rolling

Preheat the oven to 325 degrees F. In a large bowl, stir
together the butter and vanilla until well mixed. Mix in the
ingredients from the jar and stir until mixed. Roll the dough
into 1 inch balls and bake on a lightly greased cookie sheet.
Bake for 15 to 20 minutes until the bottoms are lightly
browned. Remove from cookie sheet and while warm, roll in
the confectioners' sugar.

Bakery Style Chocolate Chip Cookies

1 1/2 cups flour
1/2 teaspoon salt
1/4 teaspoon cinnamon
1/2 teaspoon baking soda
3/4 cup brown sugar, packed
1/3 cup white sugar
1 1/2 cups semi-sweet chocolate chips
Jar – Wide mouth quart glass canning jar

Mix the flour, salt, cinnamon and baking soda together and put in jar. Pack down firmly. Add the chocolate chips, brown sugar and white sugar in layers. Put the sugars on top so they can be removed separately for the recipe. Seal jar.

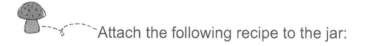

Attach the following recipe to the jar:

Bakery Style Chocolate Chip Cookies

2 1/4 teaspoons vanilla extract
1 egg
1 egg yolk
1/2 cup butter, melted

Preheat the oven to 325 degrees F. Remove the white and brown sugar from the jar (top 2 layers) and place in a large bowl. Add the melted butter to the sugars and stir until well mixed. Add the egg, egg yolk and vanilla and mix well until light and creamy. Mix in the rest of the contents of the jar. Place the cookie dough by spoonfuls on a cookie sheet and flatten cookies a bit. Bake the cookies for 15 to 16 minutes or until edges are turning light brown.

Craisin Cookie Mix

2 cups flour
1 teaspoon ground cinnamon
1 1/4 teaspoons baking soda
1 1/3 cups packed brown sugar
1 cup Craisins®
Jar - wide mouth quart canning jar

Mix the flour, cinnamon and baking soda together. Layer in jar: flour mixture, brown sugar and Craisins®. Seal jar.

Attach the following recipe to the jar:

Craisin Cookies

2/3 cup margarine
1 egg
1/2 cup milk

Preheat oven to 350 degrees F. In a large bowl, stir together the margarine and milk, then add the egg. Add the contents of the jar. Stir well. Drop dough by rounded spoonfuls on an ungreased cookie sheet. Bake for 10 to 12 minutes.

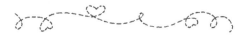

Sugar Cookie Mix

This cookie mix will fit in a pint jar.

2 cups flour
1/2 teaspoon ground cloves
1/2 teaspoon ginger
2 teaspoons baking soda
1/2 teaspoon salt
1 teaspoon cinnamon
Jar – Wide mouth pint glass canning jar

Mix together all of the above. Put in jar and seal.

 Attach the following recipe to the jar:

Sugar Cookies

3/4 cup soft margarine
1 cup sugar
1/4 cup molasses
1 egg
Extra granulated sugar for rolling

Mix together the margarine, sugar, molasses and egg, and beat well. Add the contents of the jar. Stir until well blended and chill for 1 hour or overnight.

Preheat oven to 375 degrees F. Form the cold dough into balls and roll in the cookies in sugar. (Can also be rolled in Christmas sprinkles for a more festive look.) Place on greased cookie sheet. Bake for 8 to10 minutes.

Magical Caramel Cookie Mix

1 1/3 cups flour
1/2 teaspoon baking soda
1/2 cup sugar
1/3 cup baking cocoa
1/2 cup brown sugar, packed
1/2 package Rolo candies or Hershey's Caramel Kisses
(need about 24)
Jar – Wide mouth quart glass canning jar

Combine the flour and baking soda. Layer in jar in this order: flour mixture, cocoa, sugar, brown sugar, candies. Pack each layer well except for candies and seal jar.

Attach the following recipe to the jar:

Magical Caramel Cookies

1/2 cup margarine, softened
1 egg
1 1/2 teaspoons vanilla
Sugar for rolling cookies in

Preheat oven to 375 degrees F. Remove the candies from the jar, unwrap each one and set aside. In a large bowl, combine the egg, margarine and vanilla. Add the rest of the contents of the jar to the bowl and stir well. Using about a tablespoon of dough, shape it around each candy covering the candy completely, then roll the dough in granulated sugar. Place on an ungreased cookie sheet. Bake for 7 to 10 minutes or until top is barely cracked. Makes 24 cookies.

Chocolate Mint Cookie Mix

2 cups flour
1 1/2 teaspoons baking powder
1/2 teaspoon salt
2 tablespoons cocoa
1 cup white sugar
1/4 cup mint-chocolate chips
1/4 cup pecans, chopped
Jar – Wide mouth quart glass canning jar

Mix the flour, baking powder, salt and cocoa together. In the jar, layer the flour mixture, then all the rest of the ingredients. Seal the jar.

Attach the following recipe to the jar:

Chocolate Mint Cookies

1 egg, beaten
1 teaspoon vanilla
2 tablespoons milk
1/2 cup margarine or shortening, melted

Preheat oven to 350 degrees F. Mix together the egg, vanilla, milk and margarine in a large bowl. Add the contents of the jar and mix well. Drop by spoonfuls on a lightly greased cookie sheet. Bake for 8 to 10 minutes.

Mrs. Kringle's Chocolate Kiss Cookie Mix

1 3/4 cup flour
1/4 teaspoon salt
3/4 teaspoon baking soda
1 1/2 cup granulated sugar
1/2 cup unsweetened cocoa powder
About 20 chocolate kisses
Jar – Wide mouth quart glass canning jar

Combine the flour, salt and baking soda. Layer in jar as follows: flour mixture, cocoa powder, sugar, chocolate kisses.

Attach the following recipe to the jar:

Mrs. Kringle's Chocolate Kiss Cookies

3/4 cup butter, softened
2 eggs
1 1/2 teaspoon vanilla
Granulated sugar

Preheat oven to 350 degrees F. Unwrap the chocolate kisses. Mix together the butter, eggs and vanilla. Add the contents of the jar and mix well. Form a tablespoon of dough into a 1" ball. Roll in sugar. Place on an ungreased cookie sheet and bake for 8 to10 minutes. Place chocolate kiss in the middle of each cookie while still hot.

Thumbprint Cookie Mix

1/2 cup white sugar
2 1/4 cups flour
3/4 teaspoon salt
1 1/2 cups finely chopped walnuts
Jar – Wide mouth quart glass canning jar

Mix the flour and salt together. In the jar, layer the flour mixture, white sugar and walnuts on top. Be sure to put the nuts on top because they will need to be removed and set aside when baking. Seal the jar.

Attach the following recipe to the jar:

Thumbprint Cookies

1 1/2 teaspoons vanilla
3 eggs
1 cup butter or margarine
1/2 cup strawberry, grape or apricot preserves

Preheat oven to 350 degrees F. Remove the walnuts from the top layer of the jar and set aside. Separate the eggs into 2 bowls – 3 egg yolks in one and 3 egg whites in the other. In a large bowl, mix the butter, egg yolks and vanilla together. Add the rest of the ingredients from the jar and mix well. Shape the cookies into small balls about 3/4". Dip each one in the egg whites and then roll it in the nuts. Place on a lightly greased cookie sheet and press down on each cookie with your thumb. Bake for 15 to 17 minutes. Fill the thumbprints on the cookie with preserves when cool.

Popcorn Seasoning

Cheesy Popcorn Spice Mix

1/2 cup grated parmesan cheese
2 teaspoons salt
1 teaspoon dried tarragon
1 teaspoon parsley flakes
1 teaspoon garlic powder
Jar – Wide mouth half-pint glass canning jar

Combine all ingredients in a small bowl; stir until well blended. Put in a half-pint jar.

Attach the following recipe to the jar:

Cheesy Popcorn Spice

1/4 cup margarine

To serve – Pop 3 cups of popcorn. Melt 1/4 cup margarine in a small pan over low heat. Stir in 1 tablespoon popcorn spice. Pour over popcorn and mix well.

Chocolate Popcorn Spice Mix

1/2 cup confectioner's sugar
1/4 cup mini semi-sweet chocolate chips
1 tablespoon plus 2 teaspoons cocoa
1/2 teaspoon ground cinnamon
Jar – Wide mouth half-pint glass canning jar

Combine all ingredients in a small bowl; stir until well blended. Put in half-pint jar and seal.

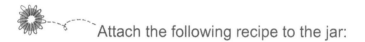 Attach the following recipe to the jar:

Chocolate Popcorn Spice

To serve, melt 1/4 cup margarine or butter in a saucepan over low heat. Stir in 2 tablespoons popcorn spice. Pour over 3 cups popped corn; mix well.

Cajun Popcorn Spice Mix

4 teaspoons paprika
4 teaspoons thyme
4 teaspoons basil
4 teaspoons cumin
1 teaspoon onion powder
4 teaspoons garlic powder
2 tablespoons salt
2 teaspoons black pepper
Optional – 1 teaspoon cayenne pepper
Jar – Wide mouth half-pint glass canning jar

Combine all ingredients in a small bowl; stir until well
blended.

Attach the following recipe to the jar:

Cajun Popcorn Spice

2 tablespoons vegetable oil

To serve – Pop 3 cups of popcorn. Heat the oil in a small
pan over medium heat for about a minute, then add about 1
tablespoon of the popcorn spice in the jar. Cook and stir for
another minute. Pour over popcorn and mix well.

Coffee, Tea, Cocoa

Peach Tea Mix

1/2 cup instant tea mix
1 cup white sugar
1/2 box of peach-flavored gelatin (3 ounces)
Jar – Wide mouth pint glass canning jar

In a bowl, combine all the ingredients and stir well. Put in a pint glass jar and seal.

Attach the following recipe to the jar:

Peach Tea

To make peach tea, stir 2 teaspoons of tea mix into 8 ounces hot water.

Spiced Hot Tea Mix

1 1/4 cups Tang or other orange breakfast drink dry mix
3/4 cup iced tea mix with lemon and sugar
1/4 teaspoon ground cloves
1 teaspoon ground cinnamon
1/2 teaspoon ground allspice
Jar – Wide mouth pint glass canning jar

In a bowl, combine all the ingredients and stir well. Put in a pint glass jar and seal.

Attach the following recipe to the jar:

Spiced Hot Tea

To make spiced tea, stir 2 teaspoons of tea mix into 8 ounces hot water.

Café Au Lait Mix

1 1/2 cups instant non-dairy creamer
1/4 cup instant coffee crystals
1/4 cup packed brown sugar
Dash salt
Jar – Wide mouth pint glass canning jar

In a bowl, combine all the ingredients and stir well. Put in a pint glass jar and seal.

Attach the following recipe to the jar:

Café Au Lait

In a cup, combine 1/4 cup of the Café Au Lait mix with 2/3 cup boiling water.

Cinnamon Mocha Mix

2 cups sweetened cocoa mix
1/3 cup instant coffee crystals
1 teaspoon ground cinnamon
Jar – Wide mouth pint glass canning jar

In a bowl, combine all the ingredients and stir well. Put in a pint glass jar and seal.

Attach the following recipe to the jar:

Cinnamon Mocha

In a cup, combine 2 tablespoons of the Cinnamon Mocha mix with 2/3 cup boiling water.

Hot Chocolate Mix

2 cups instant nonfat dry milk
1/2 cup unsweetened cocoa powder
1 cups sugar
1/4 teaspoon salt
Jar – Wide mouth quart glass canning jar or 2 pint canning jars

In a bowl, combine all the ingredients and stir well. Put in a quart or 2 pint glass jars and seal.

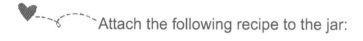Attach the following recipe to the jar:

Hot Chocolate

Combine 1/4 cup of the hot chocolate mix with a cup of boiling water.

Cafe Mocha Coffee Mix

3/4 cup unsweetened cocoa powder
3/4 cup sugar
1/4 cup instant nonfat dry milk
Jar – Wide mouth pint glass canning jar

In a bowl, combine all the ingredients and stir well. Put in a pint glass jar and seal.

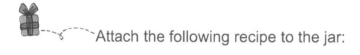Attach the following recipe to the jar:

Cafe Mocha Coffee

Combine 2 to 3 tablespoons of the Cafe Mocha mix with a cup of hot coffee.

Holly Jolly Coffee Mix

2/3 cup instant nonfat dry milk
2/3 cup sugar
1/2 cup instant coffee
1/2 teaspoon cinnamon
Jar – Wide mouth pint glass canning jar

In a bowl, combine all the ingredients and stir well. Put in a pint glass jar and seal.

Attach the following recipe to the jar:

Holly Jolly Coffee

Combine 2 teaspoons of the Holly Jolly coffee mix with a cup of hot water.

Jack Frost's Hot Orange Drink Mix

1 10-ounce jar of Tang or other orange breakfast drink dry mix
2 cups sugar
1/4 cup of lemonade mix
2 teaspoon cinnamon
1 teaspoon cloves
Jar – Wide mouth quart glass canning jar or 2 pint jars

In a bowl, combine all the ingredients and stir well. Put in a quart or 2 pint glass jars and seal.

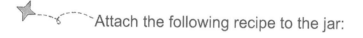Attach the following recipe to the jar:

Jack Frost's Hot Orange Drink

Combine 2 1/2 teaspoons of the hot orange drink mix with a cup of boiling water.

Fireside Coffee Mix

2/3 cup non-dairy coffee creamer
1/2 cup carnation hot cocoa mix
1/2 cup instant coffee
1/2 cup sugar
1/3 teaspoon cinnamon
1/4 teaspoon nutmeg
Jar – Wide mouth pint glass canning jar

In a bowl, combine all the ingredients and stir well. Put in a pint glass jar and seal.

Attach the following recipe to the jar:

Fireside Coffee

Combine 2 tablespoons plus 1 teaspoon of the Fireside coffee mix with a cup of boiling water.

Hot Chocolate Mix With Marshmallows

2 cups instant nonfat dry milk
3/4 cup white sugar
1/2 cup unsweetened cocoa powder
1 teaspoon cinnamon
1 cup mini marshmallows
Jar – Wide mouth quart glass canning jar

Mix the sugar, dry milk, cocoa and cinnamon together. Put in canning jar and pack. Add the mini marshmallows on top. Seal jar.

Attach the following recipe to the jar:

Hot Chocolate Mix With Marshmallows

Combine 1/4 cup of the hot chocolate mix with a cup of boiling water.

Soups

Split Pea Soup Mix

2 cups dry milk powder
1 tablespoon minced onion flakes
1 teaspoon parsley flakes
1/4 teaspoon garlic powder
1/4 teaspoon salt
1/2 teaspoon pepper
1 bay leaf
16 ounces dried split peas
Jar – Wide mouth quart glass canning jar

Combine the dry milk powder and all the ingredients above except the peas and bay leaf. Layer in the jar - first the milk mixture, then the peas and the bay leaf on top. Seal jar.

Attach the following recipe to the jar:

Split Pea Soup

2 cups diced fully cooked ham
1 to 1 1/2 cups sliced baby carrots
7 cups boiling water

Pour the contents of the jar into a crock pot. Add the boiling water. Add the carrots. Cover and cook on medium high for about 5 hours. (If your crockpot dial is 1 to 5, set it at 4) Be sure to stir occasionally. Add the cooked ham after 4 hours. Add more water if necessary while it cooks.

Chicken Rice Soup Mix

3 cups uncooked long grain brown rice
3/4 cup chicken bouillon granules
2 tablespoons dried parsley
4 tablespoons dried tarragon
1 1/2 teaspoons pepper
Jar – Wide mouth quart glass canning jar

Combine all the ingredients above and put in quart jar. Seal jar.

Attach the following recipe to the jar:

Chicken Rice Soup

4 1/2 cups water
2 tablespoons margarine
Cooked chicken pieces, optional

Bring the water, margarine and 1 cup of the soup mix in the jar to a boil. Reduce heat, cover and simmer for 40 minutes or until the rice is tender. Add cooked chicken while simmering, if desired.

Bean Soup Mix

The small jewelry bags with Ziploc tops you can find at hobby stores are perfect for the spice packet created below. Or use a small plastic container for the spices.

1 cup dried split peas
1 cup barley
1 cup dry lentils
1 cup uncooked brown or white rice
2 tablespoons parsley
1 teaspoon black pepper
2 teaspoons salt
2 tablespoons dry minced onion
2 teaspoons beef bouillon
2 teaspoons garlic powder
2 teaspoons Italian seasoning
2 teaspoons cumin
Jar – Wide mouth quart glass canning jar

Layer the first 4 ingredients in a jar. Mix all the spices together and create a spice packet in a small jewelry or Ziploc bag. Seal the jar and set the spice packet aside to attach to the outside of the jar when you attach the recipe.

 Attach the following recipe to the jar:

Bean Soup

Pour the contents of the jar into a strainer and rinse. Move the contents of the strainer to a large pot and add 12 cups of water and the spice packet. Bring the soup to a boil and then lower the heat. Cover the pot and simmer for 1 hour or more, stirring occasionally. More water may need to be added.

Potato Soup Mix

The consistency of this soup is a little thinner than most thick potato soups. But It is a great tasting soup nonetheless.

2-1/3 cups instant mashed potato flakes
2 cups dry milk powder
3 teaspoons chicken bouillon granules
1 teaspoon onion powder
1-1/4 teaspoons dried parsley
1/4 teaspoon ground pepper
1/2 teaspoon garlic powder
1 teaspoon seasoning salt
2 tablespoons dried chives
Jar – Wide mouth quart glass canning jar

Mix all the ingredients in a bowl. Pour into the jar.

Attach the following recipe to the jar:

Potato Soup

To serve, add one cup of boiling water to 1/2 cup of the soup mix in a bowl, and stir until smooth. Serve with chives, crumbled bacon, grated cheese and sour cream if desired.

Chili

Easy Vegetarian Chili Mix

By putting the chili spices in individual containers, the recipient can add as much or as little of a spice as they want. Also add the cans of beans, tomatoes and veggie flavor packets so they will have everything they need to make the chili. Use little pieces of tin foil to mix the spices, then bend the foil into little funnels and fill the small jars. Labels are available online for the cans.

2 packets Swanson vegetable flavor boost
6 ounce can of tomato paste
2 cans ranch style beans, drained and rinsed
1 can petit diced tomatoes – 28 ounces

Little jar one:
1/4 teaspoon red pepper
1 tablespoon chili powder

Little jar two:
1/3 teaspoon cumin
1 teaspoon oregano
1/2 teaspoon garlic powder
1/2 teaspoon salt

Little jar three:
1 tablespoon dried onion

Little jar four:
3 tablespoons masa flour

Jars – small glass jars (from a hobby store) or small plastic containers

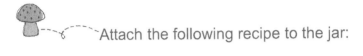Attach the following recipe to the jar:

Easy Vegetarian Chili

In a pot, combine the vegetable packets and 1 cup of water. Add all the rest of the ingredients, cover and cook on low for 4 to 6 hours. This chili can also be cooked in a crock pot.

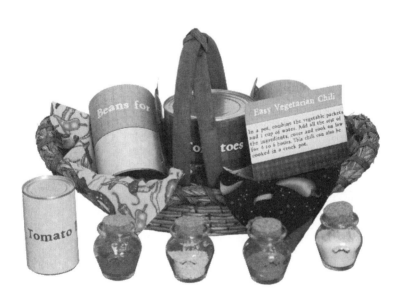

Cold Weather Chili Mix

1 tsp. salt
1/4 tsp. oregano
1 tsp. chili powder
1/4 tsp. paprika
1/2 tsp. garlic salt
1 tablespoon dried onion
Jars – several very small jars or one half-pint jar

If using a half-pint jar, mix all the spices together. Otherwise combine spices to fit in the smaller jars you are using.

 Attach the following recipe to the jar:

Cold Weather Chili

1 pound of hamburger
1 can of pinto beans or ranch style beans
1 quart tomatoes
1 can tomato soup

Brown hamburger and drain. Add all the rest of the ingredients plus the contents of the jar. Simmer about 1 hour.

Quick and Spicy Chili Mix

1 teaspoon dried onion flakes
1 teaspoon garlic powder
1 1/2 teaspoons red pepper
2 tablespoons chili powder
3/4 teaspoon salt
1/2 teaspoon black pepper
Jars – several very small jars or one half-pint jar

If using a half-pint jar, mix all the spices together. Otherwise combine spices to fit in the smaller jars you are using.

Attach the following recipe to the jar:

Quick and Spicy Chili

1 pound lean hamburger
Small can of corn, 8 ounces
1 can pinto beans, 15 ounces
Can of tomato paste, 6 ounces
Can of tomato sauce, 8 ounces
1 jalapeno pepper, chopped (optional)

Brown the hamburger and drain. In a large pot, mix the corn, beans, tomato paste, tomato sauce and one cup of water. Add the contents of the jar. Bring to a boil and then reduce heat to medium-low. Mix in the cooked hamburger. Cook 45 minutes to 1 hour, stirring occasionally.

Nuts & Snacks

Hollandaise Snack Mix

1 cup unsalted dry-roasted peanuts
1 cup Ritz bits crackers
1 cup stick pretzels
1/2 cup butter
1 teaspoon garlic powder
1 package hollandaise sauce mix, .9 ounces
1 tablespoon Worcestershire sauce
Jar – Wide mouth quart glass canning jar

Preheat oven to 300 degrees F. In a small saucepan, melt butter over medium heat. Stir in the garlic powder, hollandaise sauce and Worcestershire sauce. In a large bowl, mix together the crackers, peanuts and pretzels. Pour the butter mixture over the dry mixture. Toss until well coated.

Spread evenly on a baking sheet. Bake 15 to 20 minutes, stirring occasionally. Remove from baking sheet to cool. Spread on waxed paper or foil to cool, about 15 minutes. When completely cool, pack in quart jar and seal.

Ranch Oyster Crackers

It takes 2 cups of these to fill a pint glass canning jar, 4 cups to fill a quart glass canning jar. This recipe makes 6 cups so it will fill 3 pint jars or 1 quart and 1 pint jars.

1 package oyster crackers (12 ounces)
1/2 cup vegetable oil
1/2 teaspoon dried dill weed
1 envelope Hidden Valley® ranch dry salad dressing mix
Jar – Wide mouth pint or quart glass canning jar

Preheat oven to 200 degrees F. In a large bowl, combine Hidden Valley® seasoning, oil and dill weed. Mix well and add crackers. Toss until well coated. Spread the seasoned oyster crackers on a cookie sheet and bake for 15 to 20 minutes, stirring once halfway through. Let cool before packing in jars.

Tip: If you line the cookie sheet with parchment paper before baking, you can just slide the paper off onto the counter to let the crackers cool.

Granola

This recipe will fill about 3 quart jars.

1 cup brown sugar packed
1/2 cup water
4 teaspoon vanilla
8 cups uncooked old fashioned oatmeal
2 cups pecans and almonds
2 cups any dried fruit
Jars – 3 wide mouth quart glass canning jars

Preheat oven to 275°. Mix sugar and water together. Place in microwave safe bowl and microwave on medium high for 5 minutes. Add vanilla. Place oats and nuts in large bowl. Pour syrup mixture over oats and nuts and mix well.

Place mixture on 2 ungreased jelly roll pans. Bake for 45 to 60 minutes; stirring and tuning every 15 minutes. Cool and then add dried fruit. Fill quart jars when cooled and seal.

Hurricane Snacks

Using red and green M&M's® at Christmas will make this snack jar look festive. Use the all-colored M&M's® for a colorful jar the rest of year. A bag of just red M&M's® and just green M&M's® can be purchased online if you can't find the holiday colors anywhere else. This recipe is easy enough for the kids to make for gifts.

1 cup dry roasted peanuts
1 1/4 cups M&M's®
1 cup chocolate covered peanuts
1 (5 ounce) bag of Craisins®
Jar – Wide mouth quart glass canning jar or 2 pint canning jars

This snack can be packed one of two ways – the first, just mix the roasted and chocolate peanuts, M&M's® and Craisins® together in a large bowl and fill a quart jar. The second, layer each ingredient in a jar without mixing anything.

Reindeer Chow

1 1/2 cup semi-sweet chocolate chips
1/2 cup peanut butter
1 (15 oz.) box Rice Chex or Crispix
1 1/2 cup powdered sugar
1/4 cup margarine
Jar – Wide mouth quart glass canning

Melt the chocolate chips, peanut butter, and margarine together. Pour Rice Chex into a very large bowl. When the chocolate mixture has melted, pour over Rice Chex, stirring gently to coat. Add powdered sugar.

Cover the bowl, shake gently to coat. Pour out in single layer to dry and put in quart jar when cool.

Snack Scrabble

6 teaspoons margarine
1/2 teaspoon onion salt
1/2 teaspoon Lawry's® seasoned salt or garlic salt
4 teaspoons Worcestershire sauce
4 cups Chex cereal any combination, wheat, corn or rice
1 small package pretzels
1 can mixed nuts
Jar – Wide mouth quart glass canning jar

Preheat oven to 250°. Melt margarine and add the salts and Worcestershire sauce. Put cereal, nuts and pretzels into a 9 x 13 pan. Pour sauce over cereal and mix until coated. Bake for 45 minutes stirring every 15 minutes. Drain on paper towels.

Mixed Spiced Nuts

1 egg white, slightly beaten
2/3 cup whole almonds
2 cups dry roasted peanuts
3/4 cup sugar
2/3 cup walnut halves
3/4 teaspoon salt
1 teaspoon of pumpkin pie spice
1 teaspoon of water
Jar – Wide mouth quart glass canning jar

Preheat oven to 300 degrees F. Combine egg white and water together. Add the nuts and toss to coat. Combine the pumpkin pie spice, sugar and salt. Add this to the nuts and toss until the nuts are coated.

Spread evenly on a greased baking sheet. Bake for 20 to 25 minutes. Cool nuts on waxed paper. Break up any large clusters. Pour out in single layer to cool on wax paper and put in jar when cool.

Spicy Chili Peanuts

These will fill 2 pint canning jars.

36 ounces of cocktail peanuts (or 4 cups)
1 package chili seasoning mix (1 5/8 ounces)
1/2 cup margarine, melted
Jars – 2 wide mouth pint glass canning jars

Put the peanuts in a crockpot. Pour melted margarine over the nuts, then sprinkle with the chili mix. Toss until well mixed. Cover and cook on low for 2 to 2 1/2 hours.

Remove the crockpot lid and cook the nuts on high for 10 to 15 minutes. Pour out in single layer to cool on wax paper and put in jar when cool.

Holiday Candied Pecans

4 cups pecan halves
1 tablespoon cinnamon
1 teaspoon salt
1 egg white
2 tablespoons water
Jar – Wide mouth quart glass canning jar or 2 pint jars

Preheat oven to 250 degrees. Mix the water and egg white together in a bowl. Mix the salt and cinnamon together in another bowl.

Dip the pecans in the egg white mixture with a slotted cooking spoon, then dip the pecans into the dry mixture and shake off excess. Place them on a cookie sheet lined with parchment paper and bake for 1 hour, stirring them every 15 minutes. Cool and pack in jars.

Santa's Spiced Walnuts

4 cups of walnuts
1 cup sugar
1/4 teaspoon nutmeg
1/4 teaspoon ginger
1 teaspoon cinnamon
1/4 cup water
Jar – Wide mouth quart glass canning jar or 2 pint jars

Add water, spices and sugar to a large skillet. Bring to a boil and cook until the mixture thickens. Remove from heat. Add the walnuts to the pan and coat with mixture.

Spread the nuts out on wax paper, separate them and let them cool. After nuts are cool, pack in jars and seal.

Spicy Football Snack

2/3 cup Wheat Chex®
2/3 cup Corn Chex®
2/3 cup Cheerios®
2/3 cup Cheez-It®
2/3 cup pretzels
2/3 cup mixed nuts
1/3 cup margarine
3/4 teaspoon garlic powder
1 tablespoon Worcestershire sauce
Jar – Wide mouth quart glass canning jar

Preheat oven to 225 degrees F. Combine the first 6 ingredients in a large bowl and set aside.

Melt margarine in microwave. Add the garlic powder and Worcestershire sauce to the margarine and stir until well blended. Pour over the dry mixture and stir until the dry mixture is evenly coated.

Spread the cereal mixture on a cookie sheet. Bake for 1 hour, stirring occasionally. Cool on wax paper or parchment paper. Pack in jar when cool.

Spicy Almonds

1 egg white
4 teaspoons sugar
3 teaspoons garlic salt
1 1/2 teaspoons black pepper
1/2 teaspoon red pepper
2 teaspoons ground cumin
1 teaspoon chili powder
3 1/2 cups whole almonds with the skins on
Jar – Wide mouth quart glass canning jar or 2 pint jars

Preheat oven to 275 degrees F. Beat 1 egg white in large bowl until frothy. Add the sugar, garlic salt, red pepper, black pepper, cumin, chili powder and almonds with skins. Stir to coat almonds evenly and place almonds in single layer on a greased cookie sheet.

Bake for 40 minutes, stirring every 10 minutes. Remove from oven and cool. When cool, pack in jars.

Ranch Snack Mix

1 cup miniature pretzels
1 cup Bugles or Chex
1 cup salted cashews
1 cup bite-size cheddar cheese fish crackers
1/2 cup vegetable oil
1 envelope ranch salad dressing mix
Jar – Wide mouth quart glass canning jar

Combine pretzels, cashews, Bugles and crackers in a large bowl. Sprinkle with salad dressing mix and toss to mix. Drizzle with oil and mix until well coated. Spread on waxed paper or foil to dry before packing in jars.

Super Spicy Pecans

4 cups pecan halves
3 tablespoons margarine
3 tablespoons Worcestershire sauce
1/4 teaspoon garlic powder
1 teaspoon salt
1/2 teaspoon cinnamon
1/4 teaspoon cayenne pepper
Dash of bottled pepper sauce
Jar – Wide mouth quart glass canning jar

Preheat oven to 300 degrees F. In a heavy skillet, melt the margarine. Stir in the rest of the ingredients except nuts and mix well.

Add the pecans and stir until nuts are coated well. Bake for 20 - 25 minutes until nuts turn crispy and brown, stirring often. Let cool before packing in jar.

Dried Fruit

Use 26 ounces of dried fruit, such as dried banana chips, apricots, cranberries, pineapple, papaya and raisins.

The packages of dried fruit that weigh between 5 ounces and 7 ounces are perfect.

Jar – Wide mouth quart glass canning jar

Layer the dried fruit in a canning jar. 5 or 6 different types of dried fruit is sufficient and the colorful the better. Seal the jar.

White Chocolate Pretzel Mix

1 1/4 cups crisp rice cereal
1 1/4 cups salted peanuts
1 1/4 cups pretzel sticks
10 1-ounce squares white baking chocolate
2 teaspoons margarine
Jar – Wide mouth quart glass canning jar

Combine the cereal, peanuts and pretzels in a large bowl. Melt the chocolate and margarine in the microwave, stirring until melted. Pour over dry mixture and mix to coat evenly. Drop by heaping spoonfuls on waxed paper. Let cool before packing in jars.

Trail Mix

2 2/3 cups Honey-oat Cheerios®
3/4 cup peanuts
1/3 cup dried cranberries
1/3 cup carob chips
1/4 cup sunflower seeds
Jar – Wide mouth quart glass canning jar

Mix all the ingredients together in a large bowl and fill a quart jar. Seal the jar.

Honey Cranberry Snack Mix

This recipe fills 2 quart jars or 4 pints and makes up very quickly.

1/4 cup Jif® Creamy Peanut Butter & Honey
1/4 cup butter
1/2 teaspoon vanilla
1 teaspoon ground cinnamon
4 cups Honey Nut Chex®
1 cup mini pretzels
1 cup honey roasted peanuts
1 cup dried cranberries
Jar – 2 wide mouth quart glass canning jar

Heat oven to 350 degrees F. Mix peanuts, cereal, cranberries and pretzels in a large bowl. Have the cinnamon and vanilla ready to add. Combine butter and peanut butter in a microwave-safe bowl. Microwave on high for 25 seconds. Remove from microwave and add the cinnamon and vanilla. Stir quickly until well blended. Microwave for another 10 seconds. Pour half the hot mixture over the dry cereal mixture, stir, then add the other half of the hot mixture and still until well coated.

Line a cookie sheet with foil. Spread the mixture evenly on cookie sheet. Bake for 5 minutes, stir and bake for another 5 minutes. Transfer the mixture to a clean piece of tin foil to cool. Let cool before packing in jars.

Almond Bark Snack Mix

This recipe makes enough to fill 3 quart jars. This mix should be left loose in the jars, rather than packed. I took these snacks to work and they are still asking for more.

2 cups chocolate Chex® cereal
1 cup Honey Nut Cheerios®
1 cup mini pretzels
1 cup pecan halves
1 cup honey roasted peanuts
1 cup M&M's®
1 package almond bark (12 ounces)
Jar – 3 wide mouth quart glass canning jars

In a large bowl, combine the pretzels, nuts and cereal. In a bowl, microwave the almond bark at 50% power for 1 minute. Stir and microwave for 1 more minute at 50% power. Stir almond bark until mixed and pour over the cereal mixture, stirring until coated evenly.

Spread on wax paper or parchment paper until cool. Break into pieces. Let cool before packing in jars. Either add M&M's® before filling jars, or layer half the snack mix, then the M&M's®, then the rest of the snack mix.

Almond Bark Snack layers *not* mixed in jar

Almond Bark Snack layers mixed in jar

Muffins

Muffin Brownie Mix

1 cup all-purpose flour
1 3/4 cups sugar
1 1/4 cup chopped pecans
3/4 cups semi-sweet chocolate chips
Jar – Wide mouth quart glass canning jar

Layer the flour, chips, sugar and pecans in a jar, packing the flour and sugar layers, ending with the chocolate chips. Be sure to put the chocolate chips on top. Seal jar.

Attach the following recipe to the jar:

Muffin Brownies

1 cup margarine, melted
4 slightly beaten eggs
1 teaspoon vanilla

Preheat oven to 325 degrees F. Carefully remove just the chocolate chips from the jar. Melt chocolate chips and margarine over medium heat or microwave. Cool. Stir in vanilla, eggs and the remaining contents of the jar. Spoon batter into greased or paper-lined muffin tins. Bake about 30 minutes or until toothpick inserted in center comes out clean.

Spiced Applesauce Muffin Mix

1 1/2 cups flour
1 teaspoon cinnamon
1 teaspoon allspice
2 teaspoons baking powder
1/2 teaspoon baking soda
2/3 cup brown sugar
1/2 cup raisins
Jar – Wide mouth pint glass canning jar

Mix the flour, spices, baking powder and soda together.
Layer the flour mixture, sugar then raisins in the jar. Seal jar.

Attach the following recipe to the jar:

Spiced Applesauce Muffins

1/2 cup margarine
2 eggs
1 cup applesauce
1/4 teaspoon vanilla

Preheat oven to 350 degree F. In a large bowl, mix together the margarine, vanilla and eggs and beat until smooth. Mix in the contents of the jar. Stir until well blended. Mix in the applesauce. Line a muffin pan with paper liners. Pour the batter into muffin cups and fill about 2/3 full. Bake for 20 to 25 minutes until toothpick inserted comes out clean.

Double Chocolate Muffin Mix

1 2/3 cups flour
1/2 teaspoon baking soda
1/4 teaspoon salt
1 3/4 teaspoons baking powder
1/3 cup cocoa powder
1 1/4 cups white sugar
3/4 cup chocolate chips
1/2 cup chopped walnuts
Jar – Wide mouth quart glass canning jar

Mix the flour, baking soda, baking powder and salt together. Layer the flour mixture, the cocoa powder, white sugar, chocolate chips and walnuts in the jar. Seal jar.

Attach the following recipe to the jar:

Double Chocolate Muffins

1 cup milk
1 egg
2 tablespoons vegetable oil
3/4 teaspoon vanilla

Preheat oven to 350 degrees F. In a large bowl, mix together the milk, egg, vanilla and oil. Add the contents of the jar and mix well. Line muffin cups with paper muffin liners or grease the muffin cups. Fill the muffin cups 3/4 full. Bake for 20 to 25 minutes or until toothpick inserted comes out clean.

Apple Spice Muffin Mix

With this jar recipe, be sure to put the dried apples on the very top. Since they don't pack, anything you put on top of them (like sugar) will just fall down into the apples and the apples actually disappear from the outside of the jar.

2 cups flour
2 teaspoons baking powder
1 teaspoon allspice
1 teaspoon cinnamon
1/2 teaspoon salt
1/2 cup sugar
1/4 cup brown sugar
1 cup chopped dried apple
Jar – Wide mouth quart glass canning jar

Mix the flour, baking powder, allspice, cinnamon and salt together. Layer the flour mixture, brown sugar, white sugar and apples in the jar. Seal jar. *(Note: The brown sugar can be built up on the front of the jar for display since there isn't much brown sugar.)*

Attach the following recipe to the jar:

Apple Spice Muffins

1 egg, beaten
1/4 cup vegetable oil

3/4 cup milk

Preheat oven to 400 degrees F. Mix together the egg, milk and vegetable oil. Add the contents of the jar into the bowl and mix well. Grease muffin cups or use paper muffin liners and fill about 3/4 full. Bake 15 to18 minutes or until golden brown.

Apple Spice Muffins

Chocolate Chip Muffin Mix

2 3/4 cups flour
1 tablespoon and 1 teaspoon baking powder
3/4 teaspoon salt
2/3 cup white sugar
1 cup semi-sweet chocolate chips
Jar – Wide mouth quart glass canning jar

Combine the flour, salt and baking powder. Layer in jar in this order: flour mixture, sugar then chocolate chips in jar. Seal jar.

Attach the following recipe to the jar:

Chocolate Chip Muffins

1 cup milk
1 egg
1/3 cup vegetable oil
Topping: 3 tablespoons white sugar, 3 tablespoons brown sugar

Preheat oven to 400 degrees F. Mix the oil, egg and milk in a large bowl. Add contents of jar and stir well. Lightly grease muffin tins or line with baking cups. Fill muffin cups 2/3 full. Mix the white sugar and brown sugar (topping) together and sprinkle on top of the muffins before baking. Bake for 20 to 25 minutes or until toothpick inserted comes out clean.

Chocolate Chip Muffins

Harvest Muffin Mix

1 1/2 cups flour
1/4 teaspoon nutmeg
1 teaspoon cinnamon
1 1/2 teaspoon baking powder
1/4 teaspoon salt
1/4 teaspoon baking soda
1/2 teaspoon ginger
1/4 cup and 2 tablespoons brown sugar
1/4 cup and 2 tablespoons white sugar
1/2 cup dried cranberries, chopped
1/2 cup dried apple, chopped
1/4 cup toasted hazelnuts, chopped
1/4 cup dried figs, chopped
Jar – Wide mouth quart glass canning jar

In a large bowl, stir together the flour, baking soda, baking powder, salt, cinnamon, nutmeg and ginger. Layer the flour mixture first in a jar and pack. Add the brown sugar and white sugar. Then add the fruit and nuts in layers on top. Seal jar.

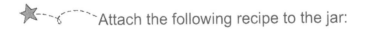Attach the following recipe to the jar:

Harvest Muffins

1/2 cup butter, melted
1 egg, beaten
1/2 cup and 2 tablespoons milk

Preheat oven to 375 degrees F. Grease muffin pans or line with paper muffin liners.

In a large bowl, add the contents of the jar. Make a well in the center and add the melted butter, milk and egg. Mix until smooth. Spoon the batter into the muffin pans to 3/4 full. Bake for 15 to 20 minutes or until a toothpick inserted comes out clean.

Blueberry Muffin Mix

2 cups flour
1/2 teaspoon salt
2 teaspoons baking powder
1 1/4 cups white sugar
1 cup dried blueberries
Jar – Wide mouth quart glass canning jar

In a large bowl, stir together the flour, baking powder and salt. Layer the flour mixture in a jar and pack. Add the white sugar next, then the blueberries. Seal jar.

Attach the following recipe to the jar:

Blueberry Muffins

1/2 cup butter
2 eggs
1/4 cup milk
Topping: 1/4 cup white sugar

Preheat oven to 375 degrees F. Lightly grease a muffin pan or use paper liners.

Mix butter, milk and eggs in a large bowl. Add all the ingredients from the jar.

Fill muffin cups 3/4 full and sprinkle with the (topping) 1/4 cup of sugar. Bake for 30 minutes.

Oatmeal Muffin Mix

Pack these ingredients firmly in a jar and they will all fit in a pint canning jar.

1 cup flour
1/2 teaspoon baking soda
1 teaspoon baking powder
Pinch of salt
3/4 cup Quaker oats (oatmeal)
2/3 cup brown sugar
Jar – Wide mouth pint glass canning jar

Mix the flour, baking soda, salt and baking powder. Layer the flour mixture in the jar, followed by the brown sugar and oats. Seal jar.

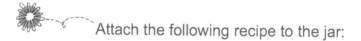 Attach the following recipe to the jar:

Oatmeal Muffins

2 eggs
1/2 cup milk
1/2 cup vegetable oil

Preheat oven to 400°. Mix eggs, milk and vegetable oil together. Add the contents of the jar and mix well. Fill muffin cups 2/3 full (use muffin liners or spray cups with vegetable oil spray). Bake for 20 minutes or until inserted toothpick comes out clean.

Bars

Apple Bars Mix

1 cup flour
3/4 teaspoon cinnamon
1/2 teaspoon baking soda
1/2 teaspoon salt
1/2 cup brown sugar
1 cup oatmeal
1 3/4 cups dried apples
1/2 cup walnuts, chopped
Jar – Wide mouth quart glass canning jar

Mix the flour, baking soda, salt and cinnamon together. In
the jar, layer the flour mixture, brown sugar, oatmeal,
walnuts and the apples on top, packing each layer. Be sure
the apples and walnuts are on top, because in the
instructions below, they will be removed from the jar and set
aside. Seal the jar.

Attach the following recipe to the jar:

Apple Bars

1/2 cup shortening
2 tablespoon margarine
1/4 cup sugar

Preheat oven to 350 degrees. Grease the bottom of an 8 or 9-inch baking pan. Remove the apples and walnuts from the jar and set aside. Empty the contents of the jar in a large bowl. Cut in the shortening until the mixture is of a crumbly texture. Evenly spread half of this crumble mixture in the bottom of the greased pan. Dot the surface with the margarine and then spread the apples in the pan. Mix the 1/4 cup sugar and the walnuts. Sprinkle the layer in the pan with the walnuts and the sugar. Finish by topping it off with the remaining half of the crumble mixture. Bake for 40 to 45 minutes.

Scratch Brownie Mix

1 1/8 cups flour
3/4 teaspoon salt
3/4 cup cocoa powder
2 1/4 cups sugar
3/4 cup semi-sweet chocolate chips
Jar – Wide mouth quart glass canning jar

Mix together the flour and salt. Layer in jar with the flour mixture first, then cocoa powder, sugar and the chocolate chips on top in case everything doesn't fit. Pack the layers well and it should all fit in the jar.

Attach the following recipe to the jar:

Scratch Brownies

3/4 cup margarine or butter, melted
3 eggs, beaten
2 1/4 teaspoons vanilla

Preheat oven to 350 degrees F. Empty the contents of the jar into a large bowl. Make a well in the center of the dry ingredients and add the margarine, vanilla and eggs. Mix well. Spread the batter into a greased 9" x 13" baking pan. Bake for 35 to 40 minutes. Cool in pan.

Raisin Carrot Bar Mix

1 package carrot cake mix
3/4 cup raisins
1/2 cup chopped walnuts
Jar – Wide mouth quart glass canning jar

Layer the ingredients above in a jar in this order –carrot cake mix, raisins, then the nuts and seal jar.

Attach the following recipe to the jar:

Raisin Carrot Bars

1/2 cup vegetable oil
1/4 cup water
2 eggs
1 can of cream cheese frosting

Preheat oven to 350°. Mix the contents of the jar, water, vegetable oil and eggs in a large bowl. Spread evenly in pan. Grease and flour a jelly roll pan, 15×10×1 inch. Bake 15 to 20 minutes or until bars spring back when touched lightly in center. Cool then frost with can of frosting. Cut into bars.

Frosted Coffee Bar Mix

3 cups flour
1/4 teaspoon salt
1 teaspoon baking powder
1 teaspoon baking soda
1 teaspoon cinnamon
2 cups brown sugar
1 cup raisins
1/2 cup nuts
Jar – Wide mouth quart glass canning jar

Mix the flour, baking soda, baking powder, salt and cinnamon together. In the jar, layer the flour mixture, brown sugar, raisins and nuts. Seal the jar.

Attach the following recipe to the jar:

Frosted Coffee Bars

1/2 cup margarine or butter
1 cup coffee
2 eggs
1 teaspoon vanilla
Powdered sugar for top

Preheat oven to 350 degrees F. In a large bowl, mix the butter and eggs together, then add the vanilla and coffee. Add the contents of the jar and mix well. Bake in 9" x 13" greased cake pan for 15 to 20 minutes.

Optional Powdered Sugar Frosting
1 1/2 cups powdered sugar
3 tablespoons butter, softened
1 tablespoon milk
1 tablespoon vanilla

Combine all the above, beating until creamy. Frost the coffee bars with a thin layer while they are still warm. Add a little more milk to thin the consistency if needed.

Note: For coffee flavor in the frosting, add 1/2 teaspoon instant coffee granules and 1 1/2 tablespoons cocoa powder to the frosting.

Chocolate Chip Squares Mix

1 cup packed brown sugar
2 cups flour
1 cup semi-sweet chocolate chips
Jar – Wide mouth quart glass canning jar

In the jar, layer the flour, brown sugar and chocolate chips in a jar, packing each layer except the chips. Seal the jar.

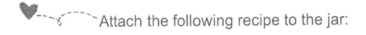Attach the following recipe to the jar:

Chocolate Chip Squares

1 cup butter, melted
1 teaspoon vanilla extract

Preheat oven to 350 degrees F. In a large bowl, mix together the melted butter or margarine and vanilla. Add the contents of the jar and mix well. Press in an ungreased jelly roll pan or cookie sheet. Bake for 20 minutes.

Butterscotch Square Mix

1 1/2 cup flour
2 teaspoons baking powder
1 cup brown sugar
1 cup white sugar
3/4 cup pecans or walnuts
Jar – Wide mouth quart glass canning jar

Mix the flour and baking powder, then layer the flour mixture, sugars and the nuts on top, being sure to pack each layer. Be sure to pack the nuts on top so they can be removed from the jar and set aside when baking.

Attach the following recipe to the jar:

Butterscotch Squares

1 cup butter, melted
2 eggs beaten
2 teaspoons vanilla

Preheat oven to 350 degrees F. Remove the nuts from the jar and set aside. Mix the eggs, butter and vanilla. Add the rest of the contents of the jar. Cover the bottom of a 9" x 13" greased pan with the nuts. Pour the mixture over nuts and bake for 20 to 30 minutes.

Coconut Chocolate Bar Mix

1 2/3 cups crushed graham crackers
1 2/3 cups shredded coconut
1/2 cup chocolate chips
Jar – Wide mouth quart glass canning jar

Layer each ingredient above in a jar and seal.

Attach the following recipe to the jar:

Coconut Chocolate Bars

1 3/4 cups sweet condensed milk

Preheat oven to 350 degrees F. Pour the contents of the jar into a large bowl. Mix well and then add the condensed milk. Stir until well blended. Grease a 9" baking pan. Press mixture evenly into the baking pan. Bake for 30 minutes.

Energy Bar Mix

1/2 teaspoon cinnamon
3/4 cup whole wheat flour
1/2 teaspoon salt
1 2/3 cups rolled oats
1/3 brown sugar, packed
1/4 cup flax seeds
1/3 cup wheat germ
1/4 sunflower seeds
1/4 sesame seeds
1/4 semi-sweet chocolate chips
Jar – Wide mouth quart glass canning jar

Mix the flour, salt and cinnamon together. Place the flour mixture in jar and then layer the rest of the ingredients. Seal the jar.

Attach the following recipe to the jar:

Energy Bars

1 egg, beaten
1/3 cup honey
1/3 cup canola oil
3/4 teaspoon vanilla

Preheat oven to 350 degrees F. Mix the egg, honey, canola oil and vanilla together in a large bowl. Add the mixture from the jar and stir until well mixed. Press the mixture into a 9" x

13" lightly greased pan. Bake for 20 to 25 minutes or until the edges are lightly browned.

Blonde Brownie Mix

2 cups flour
1 1/2 tablespoons baking powder
1/4 teaspoon salt
2/3 cup chopped pecans
1/2 cup coconut
2 cups packed brown sugar

Mix the flour, baking powder and salt together. Layer ingredients in the order above in the jar. Press each layer firmly in place.

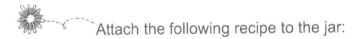Attach the following recipe to the jar:

Blonde Brownies

3/4 cup margarine
2 eggs, beaten slightly
2 teaspoons vanilla

Preheat oven to 375 degrees F. Pour the jar mixture into a large bowl and stir until mixed. Add the margarine, eggs and vanilla. Mix until blended. Spread the batter in a lightly greased 13 x 9 inch pan. Bake for 25 minutes. Cut into bars. Makes 2 dozen brownies.

Granola Coconut Bar Mix

2 cups old-fashioned oats
2/3 cup semi-sweet chocolate chips
1/2 cup packed brown sugar
1/3 cup flaked coconut
1/3 cup walnuts
1/3 cup raisins
Jar – Wide mouth quart glass canning jar

In the jar, layer all the ingredients as listed above. Seal the jar.

Attach the following recipe to the jar:

Granola Coconut Bars

1/2 peanut butter
1 1/2 teaspoons vanilla
1/3 cup honey or corn syrup
1/3 cup margarine, melted

Preheat oven to 325 degrees F. In a large bowl, combine corn syrup, peanut butter, margarine and vanilla. Add the jar of mix and stir until mixed well. Press into a greased 13 x 9 inch glass baking pan. Bake for 20 to 25 minutes. Cut into bars.

Holiday Bar Mix

3 cups Rice Krispies
1/2 cup chocolate chips
1/2 cup butterscotch chips
Jar – Wide mouth quart glass canning jar

In the jar, layer the chips, then the cereal. Be sure to put the cereal on top so they can dump the cereal out separately. Seal the jar.

Attach the following recipe to the jar:

Holiday Bars

3/4 cups peanut butter
1/2 cup light corn syrup
1/2 cup sugar

Grease bottom of a 9x13-inch cake pan. Combine peanut butter, corn syrup and sugar in a large saucepan and stir over low heat until smooth. Be sure to stir constantly to avoid burning the mixture.

Pour just the cereal from the jar into a large bowl. Pour syrup mixture over cereal and mix through. Pat into the cake pan and sprinkle the surface with the chocolate and butterscotch chips. Warm bars in the oven or microwave until chips have melted enough to spread easily over bars. Allow bars to cool then cut into squares for serving.

Raisin Peanut Bar Mix

1/4 cup firmly packed light-brown sugar
2 cups Spoon Size Shredded Wheat, crushed
3/4 cup seedless raisins
Jar – Wide mouth quart glass canning jar

Layer the brown sugar first in a jar, pack firmly, and then add the raisins. Add the shredded wheat last. The brown sugar needs to be the first packed layer so it can be separated for the recipe below.

Attach the following recipe to the jar:

Raisin Peanut Bars

1/4 cup corn syrup
1/4 cup chunky peanut butter

Empty the contents of the jar in a bowl, except the bottom brown sugar layer. The brown sugar is packed in the jar and should remain in the jar if the other ingredients are just poured out.

Combine the brown sugar (bottom layer of jar) and corn syrup in a pan. Over medium-high heat, stir until the sugar dissolves. Remove pan from heat and mix in the peanut butter. Stir in the rest of the ingredients from the jar until well coated. Press into lightly greased 8"x8" baking pan.

Chocolaty Bar Mix

2 cup all-purpose flour
1/4 teaspoon salt
1 cup brown sugar (packed)
1 cup chocolate chips
Jar - 1 wide mouth quart canning jar

Mix the flour and salt together. Layer the flour mixture, brown sugar then the chocolate chips in the jar. Be sure the chips are the last layer so they can be removed and set aside in the recipe below.

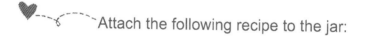Attach the following recipe to the jar:

Chocolaty Bars

1 cup butter softened
1 egg yolk
1 teaspoon vanilla

Remove the chocolate chips from the jar and set aside.

Heat oven to 350 degrees F. Grease a 9" x 13" baking pan. Mix butter, egg yolk and vanilla thoroughly. Blend in the brown sugar and flour mixture from the jar. Press evenly in bottom of pan. Bake 25 to 30 minutes until light brown. Remove from oven and immediately place the chocolate chips on top. When chocolate has softened, spread evenly over the top.

Fruit Bar Mix

3/4 cup sifted flour
1/2 teaspoon baking soda
1/2 teaspoon nutmeg
1/2 teaspoon cinnamon
1/2 teaspoon ground cloves
1/2 teaspoon salt
1 cup chopped nuts
1 cup chopped raisins
Jar – Wide mouth quart glass canning jar

Combine the flour, baking soda, nutmeg, cinnamon, cloves and salt. Layer in jar in this order: flour mixture, nuts and then raisins. Seal jar.

Attach the following recipe to the jar:

Fruit Bars

1/2 cup margarine, melted
1/2 cup molasses
2 eggs, well beaten

Preheat oven to 375 degrees F. Combine the margarine, molasses and eggs in a large bowl. Add the fruit bar mix from the jar and stir until well blended. Pour into a greased 9" x 9" baking pan. Bake for 25 to 30 minutes. Cool and cut into squares.

North Pole S'mores Mix

*When the weather outside is too cold for campfire s'mores,
here's the next best thing. This gooey sweet dessert is a
great hit with kids and Santa's helpers.*

2 cups graham cracker crumbs
1 1/2 cups miniature marshmallows
1 cup semi-sweet chocolate chips
1/8 cup sugar
Jar – Wide mouth quart glass canning jar

Layer all the above ingredients in a jar in this order: sugar,
graham cracker crumbs, chocolate chips, mini
marshmallows. Be sure chips and marshmallows are the last
layers so they can be removed and set aside in the recipe
below. Seal jar.

Attach the following recipe to the jar:

North Pole S'mores

1/2 cup margarine, melted

Preheat oven to 350 degrees F. Spray cooking spray in a 9
inch square baking dish. Remove the mini marshmallows
and chocolate chips from the jar; set aside.

Pour the rest of the contents of the jar in a large bowl and add the melted margarine. Stir until well mixed. Press half of this crumb mixture in the bottom of the baking dish and bake for 5 minutes. Layer the chocolate chips, then marshmallows on top of the graham cracker mixture. Press the remaining crumb mixture on top. Bake for 10 minutes, until the marshmallows are melted. Cool and cut into bars.

Date Nut Bar Mix

3/4 cup flour
1 cup sugar
1 cup pecans, chopped
1 cup dates, chopped
Jar – Wide mouth quart glass canning jar

Layer in jar in this order: flour, sugar, pecans, then dates.
Seal jar.

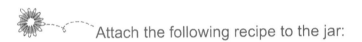 Attach the following recipe to the jar:

Date Nut Bars

1/2 cup oil
1 teaspoon vanilla
2 eggs
Powdered sugar, (optional)

Preheat oven to 350 degrees F. Mix the oil, vanilla and eggs
together with the ingredients from the jar. Pour into a 9 x 13"
baking pan. Bake for 20 minutes. Sprinkle with powdered
sugar after cutting.

Chocolate Oatmeal Bar Mix

3/4 cup brown sugar
2 cups quick cooking oats
1 1/2 cups chocolate chips
1/2 cup walnut pieces or slivered almonds
Jar – Wide mouth quart glass canning jar

Layer the brown sugar and oatmeal in the jar and pack. On top, layer the chocolate chips and walnuts, and seal. Be sure to put the chocolate chips and walnuts on top so they can be removed easily and set aside when baking.

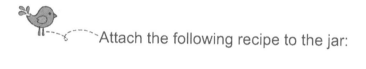Attach the following recipe to the jar:

Chocolate Oatmeal Bars

1/2 cup butter, melted
1 teaspoon vanilla

Preheat oven to 350 degrees F. Remove the nuts and chocolate chips from the jar and set aside. Combine the melted butter and vanilla in a large bowl, and then add the rest of the ingredients from the jar. Bake in 8" x 8" pan at 350° for 20 minutes. Immediately sprinkle chocolate chips on top. Let stand 5 minutes or until melted. Spread the chocolate over the bars and sprinkle with nuts.

Peanut Butter Brownie Mix

1 1/4 cup flour
1/4 teaspoon salt
1/2 teaspoon baking powder
1/2 cup cocoa
1 cup sugar
1 cup peanut butter chips
Jar – Wide mouth quart glass canning jar

Mix the flour, baking powder and salt together in a bowl. Place the flour mixture in the jar, pack, and then layer the rest of the ingredients.

Attach the following recipe to the jar:

Peanut Butter Brownies

1/4 cup corn syrup
1 teaspoon vanilla
2 eggs
3/4 cup butter

Preheat oven to 350 degrees. Mix all the ingredients in a large bowl and mix well. Add all the ingredients from the jar and stir until well mixed. Bake for 20 to 30 minutes. Frost when cool.

Optional Frosting -
1/2 cup butter
3/4 cup peanut butter
12 oz. semi-sweet chocolate chips

Put all the ingredients above in a microwavable dish and microwave on high for 1 1/2 minutes. Stir until smooth and spread over cooled brownies.

Cinnamon Coffee Cake Mix

3/4 cup sugar
1 cup flour
1 1/2 teaspoon baking powder
1/4 teaspoon salt
Jar – Wide mouth pint glass canning jar

Mix the flour, baking powder, sugar and salt together. Place the flour mixture in jar and seal the jar.

Attach the following recipe to the jar:

Cinnamon Coffee Cake

1/4 cup shortening
1 egg
1 teaspoon vanilla
1/2 cup milk
2 teaspoons butter
Cinnamon and sugar to taste

Preheat oven to 350°. Put all ingredients above in a bowl and beat till smooth. Add the contents of the jar and mix well. Pour into 9 inch pie plate and bake for approximately 20 minutes. Take out of oven and spread with butter. Sprinkle sugar and cinnamon over top.

Breads

Pumpkin Bread Mix

3 1/2 cups flour
2 teaspoons baking soda
1 1/2 teaspoons salt
1 teaspoon cinnamon
1 teaspoon allspice
1 teaspoon nutmeg
1/2 teaspoon ground cloves
Jar – Wide mouth quart glass canning jar

Mix all the ingredients above and put in canning jar.

Attach the following recipe to the jar:

Pumpkin Bread

3 cups granulated sugar
1 cup vegetable oil
4 eggs, beaten
1 lb. canned pumpkin
2/3 cup water

Preheat oven to 350 degrees. Mix sugar, oil and eggs

together. Add the can of pumpkin. Add the pumpkin bread mix from the jar, then water, stirring until mixed. Pour the batter into 2 greased and floured 9" x 5" loaf pans. Bake for 55 to 60 minutes.

Nut Bread Mix

2 cups flour
4 teaspoons baking powder
1 teaspoon salt
3/4 cup chopped walnuts
Jar – Wide mouth pint glass canning jar

Mix the flour, baking powder and salt together. Place the flour mixture in jar, then the walnuts. Seal the jar.

Attach the following recipe to the jar:

Nut Bread

1 egg, beaten
1 cup sugar
1 cup milk

Preheat oven to 325 degrees F. Mix egg, milk and sugar together in a large bowl. Add the ingredients from the jar. Stir until smooth. Pour into a buttered loaf pan. Bake for about 45 minutes.

Zucchini Bread Mix

3 cups flour
1 teaspoon baking soda
3 teaspoons cinnamon
1 teaspoon salt
1 teaspoon baking powder
1/2 cup chopped walnuts
Jar – Wide mouth quart glass canning jar

Mix all the above ingredients except walnuts. Place all in jar and seal jar.

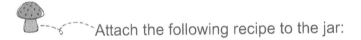Attach the following recipe to the jar:

Zucchini Bread

2 cups sugar
2 cups grated zucchini
2 teaspoons vanilla
3 eggs
1 cup vegetable oil

Preheat oven to 325 degrees F. In a large bowl, combine the eggs, sugar and oil. Add the vanilla and zucchini. Stir in the jar of zucchini bread mix until blended.

Grease and flour 2 8" x 4" loaf pans. Pour the batter evenly between the 2 pans. Bake for 55 to 65 minutes.

Pineapple Bread Mix

This recipe will make 2 pineapple bread loaves.

2 cups sifted flour
1 teaspoon baking powder
1/2 teaspoon salt
1 teaspoon baking soda
1/2 cup sugar
1 cup raisins
1/2 cup chopped nuts
Jar – Wide mouth quart glass canning jar

Combine the flour, baking powder, baking soda and salt.
Layer in jar in this order: flour mixture, sugar, nuts, raisins.
Seal jar.

Attach the following recipe to the jar:

Pineapple Bread

1 egg, slightly beaten
1 teaspoon vanilla
2 tablespoons melted margarine
1 cup crushed pineapple, well drained

Combine the egg, vanilla and margarine in a large bowl. Add
the bread mix from the jar. Stir until well blended. Add the
drained pineapple. Pour into 2 greased loaf pans. Bake 350
degrees for 50 to 60 minutes or until inserted toothpick
comes out clean.

Banana Wheat Bread Mix

This recipe makes one loaf and fits in a pint canning jar. Use a quart jar if you want to double the recipe.

2 cups whole wheat flour
1 teaspoon baking soda
1 teaspoon salt
1/2 cup chopped pecans
Jar – Wide mouth pint glass canning jar

Mix all the above ingredients together except the pecans. Place the flour mixture in jar, then the pecans. Seal jar.

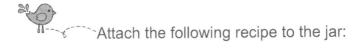Attach the following recipe to the jar:

Banana Wheat Bread

1/2 cup honey
2 eggs, beaten
1/4 cup vegetable oil
3 medium bananas, peeled
1 teaspoon vanilla

Preheat oven to 350 degrees F. Mash bananas in a bowl, and then add the rest of the ingredients above to the bananas. Put the contents of the jar in a large bowl, add the banana mixture and mix well. Pour into a greased 9" x 5" loaf pan and bake 50 to 60 minutes or until toothpick inserted near the center comes out clean.

This cute wire canning jar holder with a handle can be found at Walmart. It's perfect for gifting 2 jars.

Exclusively for *100 Easy Recipes In Jars* readers:

Over 2000 Online Labels

and Recipe Cards Available at

NorthPoleChristmas.com/jars.html

Other books by Bonnie Scott

100 Easy Camping Recipes

Now in Paperback and Kindle versions

Made in the USA
Charleston, SC
20 November 2012